101 MORE

REASONS WHY A CAT IS BETTER THAN A MAN

ALLiA ZobeL

ILLUSTRATIONS by NicoLE HoLLANDER

ADAMS MEDIA CORPORATION
Holbrook, Massachusetts

Text copyright ©1997 Allia Zobel.
Illustrations copyright ©1997 Nicole Hollander.
All rights reserved, including the right to reproduce this
book or portions thereof in any form whatsoever.
Published by Adams Media Corporation
260 Center Street, Holbrook, Massachusetts 02343

ISBN: 1-55850-794-9

A B C D E F G H I J

Printed in Korea

Library of Congress Cataloging-in-Publication Data
Zobel, Allia.
101 more reasons why a cat is better than a man /
Allia Zobel : illustrated by Nicole Hollander.
        p.   cm.
        ISBN 1-55850-749-9 (pbk.)
1. Cats—Humor. 2. Men—Humor. I. Hollander, Nicole. II. Title.
        PN6231.C23Z625   1997
        818'.5402—dc21   97-20868
                                        CIP

This book is available at quantity discounts for bulk purchases.
For information call 1 (800) 872-5627
(in Massachusetts, call (617) 767-8100).
Visit our web site at http://www.adamsmedia.com

For God; my mother, Lucille; and some of the forebearing males in my life—my husband, Desmond Finbarr Nolan; my dad, Alvin G. Zobel, Jr.; and my grandfather, Louis Frank—as well as enlightened men everywhere who have a hearty sense of humor.

And, of course, for the pride of their Mommy's life—the puddies—the dark, suave, intelligent, sweet-talking, lady-killer, Winston Stanley III ("The Thoid") and the ever-gorgeous, pristine, reserved, and elegantly sophisticated Vanessa, ("Dah-ling").

— A.Z.

To my personal Bermuda triangle: Buddy, Izzy, and Eric.

— N.H.

For Ed Walters, Donna Greer, Wayne Jackson, the Adams Media distributors, and booksellers far and near, a huge thanks for their support.

—A.Z.

Buddy, Izzy, and Eric drew all the pictures, and I would be nothing without them.

—N.H.

Introduction

When I wrote the petite, green-covered book, *101 Reasons Why A Cat Is Better Than A Man* three years ago, I thought I had found, as they say in codependent lingo, "closure." Looking back, I can even remember what I scrawled in my daily reminder the day I mailed the manuscript off: "Cat book–Finished. The end of it!!!"

Indeed, though I am generally very cautious with my use of the triple exclamation point, in that instance, I knew it was warranted. I had gotten what I had to say off my chest. It was over, done with, *fini*. That was that.

Then strange things started happening. I'd wake up in the middle of the night like a shot, reach for my pad and pen (carefully, so as not to disturb the puddies), and fill up pages with rows of sentences. "A cat would never gut a deer on the dining room table. A cat would never wear a baseball cap backward. A cat would never. . . ."

This went on for a couple of months. I was exhausted and in need of sleep. So I made an appointment with my muse, a bleach blonde cat lover named "Pixie" and asked her, point blank: "What gives?"

"You and I both know your first book was just the tip of the iceberg," said Pixie impatiently. She was chewing a wad of Hubba Bubba diet bubble gum and made it plain she was in a hurry.

"So, don't fight it," she said, snapping a bubble. "Just write it."

Then, in a puff, she disappeared.

Well, we all know there are more than 101 reasons why a cat is better than a man. And believe me, once you start making a list, it's not the kind of thing you can just walk away from. I *have* tapered off, though. And I'm hoping this book will finally put an end to it. (Let me just jot this down before I forget. . . . "A cat would never use all the hot water.") Okay, now what was I saying?

— A.Z.

P.S. Thanks to everyone who shared her/his own favorite reason with me. See, I told you this was catching!

A cat knows what color your eyes are.

Cats are laid back.

A cat would never criticize your driving.

Cats think you look terrific in a miniskirt.

A CAT WOULD NEVER MAKE FUN OF YOUR BUNNY SLIPPERS.

A cat would never compare your cooking
to his mother's.

Cats figure if you gain a few pounds, so what?
There's more of you to love!

A cat would never ask his secretary to pick out your anniversary gift.

Cats don't mention your "biological clock" in mixed company.

CATS NEVER QUESTION YOU ABOUT THE
CONTENTS OF YOUR CASSEROLES.

CATS DON'T USE UP ALL the HOT WATER.

A cat would never say "I'll give you a call,"
if he didn't mean it.

Cats don't ask you to buy life insurance
policies in their name.

A cat would never squawk about
your cell phone bill.

Cats don't leave articles about liposuction
on the kitchen table.

CATS are never Late for Dinner.

A cat would ask for directions if he were lost.

A cat wouldn't dream of buying you a
Chia Pet as a gift (unless it resembles him).

Cats never gripe about your perfume.

A cat would never break a date with you to play poker with his friends.

CATS ARE FUN IN BED.

A CAT WOULD NEVER SHAVE HIS HEAD AND WEAR AN EARRING.

Cats put you on a pedestal.

A cat would never insist you start
a pension plan.

You'd never catch a cat in a skimpy bathing suit.

Cats don't gut fish in the sink.

CATS MAKE ALLOWANCES FOR YOUR CRYING JAGS.

Cats don't have cold feet.

A cat would never leave you for
a younger woman.

Cats are not influenced by the crowd.

A cat would never put you on the speaker phone without telling you.

Cats trust you implicitly.

CATS TAKE TIME WITH MEALS.

Cats always find you exciting—no matter how many years you've been together.

Cats never show off
(unless they're in a competition).

Cats never make excuses when you invite them to the ballet.

Cats always laugh at your jokes.

A cat would never suggest a trial separation.

Cats don't make a
big deal about Superbowl Sunday, unless,
of course, you serve shrimp dip.

Cats are (generally) more understanding when you explain why you're late.

Cats aren't interested in impressing anyone—except you.

CATS COULD CARE LESS IF YOU HAVE CELLULITE.

Cats don't mind how often you entertain.

Cats don't get bent out of shape if the checkbook doesn't balance.

A cat would never wear a shirt that called attention to his chest hair.

Cats don't give you a lecture when you ask for money to go shopping.

Cats prefer the History Channel to the Playboy Channel.

A cat would never take off his collar much less his wedding ring.

You'll never get a call from your cat's ex-wife.

Cats don't have a canary if your dress is low-cut.

CATS UNDERSTAND A WOMAN'S
NEED to be CREATIVE

A cat would never take you to a wrestling match on your birthday.

Cats don't care what your politics are.

A cat would never get annoyed if you ripped
a few things from the newspaper.

A cat would never complain if you wear a face mask
and a flannel nightgown to bed.

CATS AGREE WITH YOUR TASTE IN HATS.

Cats never tire of listening to you talk about your girlfriends.

A cat would never grumble if you asked him to line-dance.

A cat would never kiss and tell.

Cats love to stare into your eyes.

A cat would follow you anywhere.
But he'll never lead you on.

CATS KNOW HOW VITAL CHOCOLATE IS TO A WOMAN'S WELL-BEING.

CATS DON'T WEAR BASEBALL CAPS BACKWARDS.

Cats are never disconcerted when you call them by their pet names.

Cats encourage you to "be yourself."

A cat doesn't care how many children you have, as long as he's your "baby."

To a cat, the only thing remotely interesting about golf is a birdie.

CATS KNOW HOW IMPORTANT it is
to tReAt YOURSELF.

A cat would never raise his eyebrow if you had a second dessert.

You are never "geographically undesirable" to a cat.

A cat would never interrupt you in the middle of a story (unless he lost his mouse).

Though he may cause it, a cat would never point out a run in your stocking.

A CAT WOULD NEVER MAKE A WISECRACK ABOUT YOUR POTTERY.

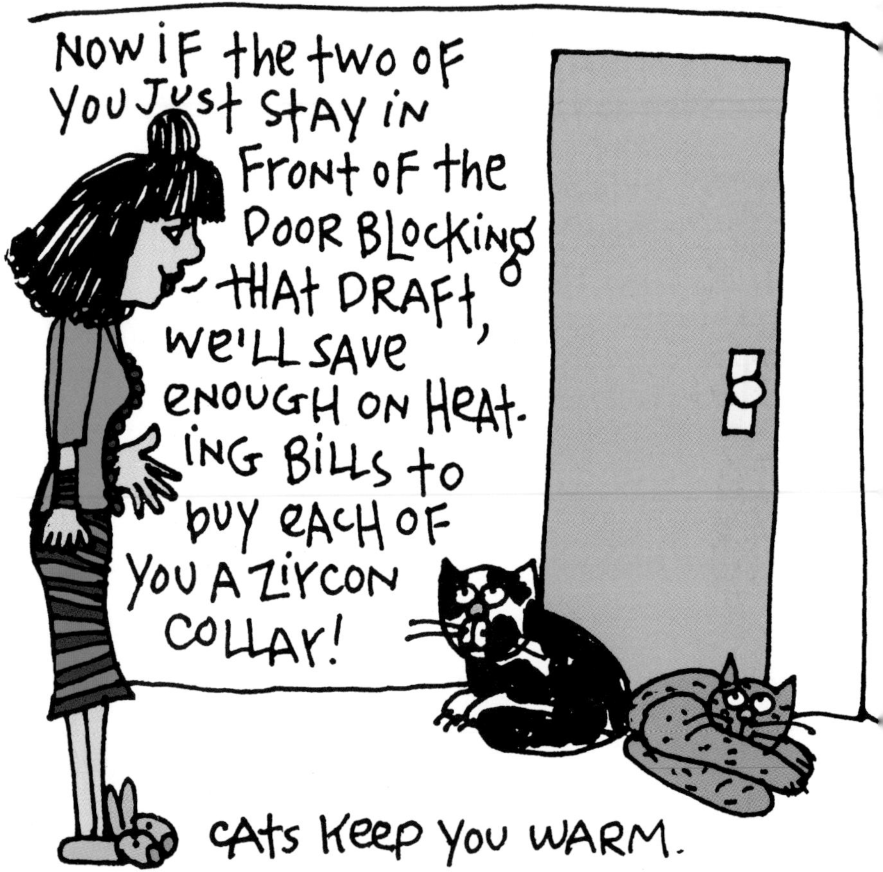

cats keep you warm.

You never have to invite your cat's mother over for the holidays.

Cats never smell of garlic, tobacco, or light beer.

A cat would never tell you your dress is too tight.

Cats don't hang gun collections
in the family room.

Cats think the gray in your hair looks chic.

Cats always close the door when they're
in the powder room.

Cats are never impatient when you
ask them questions.

Cats don't care how long it takes you
to get to the point.

Cats don't compare their muscles to other cats'.

He picked out the costume HIMSELF.

CAts Are in touch with their Feminine SiDe.

A cat would let you know if he's going to be late.

Cats are direct; they don't beat around the bush.

Cats crave your affection.

Cats adore browsing through
Modern Bride with you.

CATS MISS YOU WHEN YOU'RE AWAY.

Cats don't have problems "relating."

A cat will love you forever.

About the Author

ALLIA ZOBEL is the author of *101 Reasons Why a Cat Is Better than a Man*, *101 Reasons Why Cats Make Great Kids*, *Women Who Love Cats Too Much*, *The Joy of Being Single* and *Younger Men Are Better than Retin-A*. She lives in Bridgeport, Connecticut.

About the Illustrator

NICOLE HOLLANDER'S nationally syndicated comic strip *Sylvia* has a devoted following from coast to coast. She is also the illustrator of *101 Reasons Why a Cat Is Better than a Man*, *101 Reasons Why Cats Make Great Kids*, and *Women Who Love Cats Too Much*. Ms. Hollander lives in Chicago, Illinois.